The Accidental
Courage
of Our Lives

The Accidental Courage of Our Lives

poems

Victoria Melekian

Sheila-Na-Gig Editions

Cover photo: Victoria Melekian
Front cover design & author photo: John Farrell MacDonald

ISBN: 978-1-962405-38-6
Library of Congress Control Number: 2025944885

Sheila-Na-Gig Editions
Russell, KY
Hayley Mitchell Haugen, Editor
www.sheilanagigblog.com

For my family

Acknowledgments

805 Lit + Art: "Everything Was Going to Be Better"

A Year in Ink: "Coasting Downhill," "Going Nowhere," "Leaving Blue"

Atlanta Review: "Sentinel Node"

Autumn Sky Poetry Daily: "Hallelujah This Sky"

Better Than Starbucks: "For My Sons, A Few Facts"

Eunoia Review: "Alchemy," "Counting," "Escape to Moon Palace," "Just Because," "New Year's Eve," "Start With Beautiful" (as "Start With Beautiful and Go From There"), "The End of Me"

Fixional: "Sinking"

Front Porch Review: "Stitching" (as "Looking Back")

Green Hills Literary Lantern: "Normal"

Gyroscope Review: "Welcome Back"

LAdige Review, California Poets: "City of Angels," " Forgotten Language of Dreams," "Someone's Peeling an Orange," "Starting From Scratch," "We See the Past When We Look at Stars"

Magee Park Poets: "Feels Like Home"

Only Light Can Do That: 100 Post-Election Poems, Stories, & Essays: "Looking for Hope"

ONE ART: a journal of poetry: "My Heart Is a Shattered Windshield"

Poetry Super Highway: "Grandma's Telling Me"

Random Sample Review: "I'm Still Saving a Seat" (as "Some Things Can't Last Forever")

River Heron Review: "Redistribution," "The Accidental Courage of Our Lives"

Rust & Moth: "Wind Season in Los Angeles"

Sheila-Na-Gig online: "Quite Likely a Cerebellar Astrocytoma"

The Big Windows Review: "There's a Nest in the Purple-Flowered Tree"

The Heartland Review: "Not Yet, My Grandchildren Aren't Ready"

The Literary Nest: "Some Call It Treasure"

The Orchards Poetry Journal: "No More Lonely White Moon"
The Sunlight Press: "Katie Asks Why Not Be Optimistic,"
    "Space is Silent"
Third Wednesday: "Splintered White Picket Fence"
Verse-Virtual: "Tuesday Morning Is When I Find Out"
    (as "Diagnosis"), "Status: Post Left Breast Carcinoma"
Vine Leaves Literary Journal—A Collection of Vignettes From
    Across the Globe: "Oncology Waiting Room"
Willows Wept Review: "Colleen, Say Yes"

Contents

I.

II.

III.

I.

Windows

If forced to make a list, bad and good,
I'd say I'm good at pouring two glasses

of wine, making sure they're even.
I'm bad at math. I'm good with vocabulary words.

Bad at pronouncing them. I can parallel park
and catch falling objects. Bad at washing windows.

They're always smeared and fuzzy when I'm done,
kind of the opposite of the goal. You want

to look out windows and see the view. Or maybe not.
Maybe I'm actually good at obfuscation.

That was a word of the day from March last year.
I can barely remember this morning, but I remember

that word, and I remember it popped up in March,
a week after COVID lockdown, and I remember

devouring the news and understanding nothing
because—well, because of obfuscation.

The entire world had changed and I needed answers:
what are protein sources other than meat, how long

can I collect unemployment, is hoarding immoral.
What to do when a bird flies into a window.

Where to go when the wilderness center is shut down.
How deep do you bury a bird.

New Year's Eve

Last year's resolutions are in the garage
stuffed in a Mason jar. They send their regrets.

What's good for today might not be best in March,
say, or August when the hot summer sun

is beating down my resolve to clean up
the debris in my life. I'm older than I ever

thought I'd be, and maybe that's enough.
Anyone who deserved an apology got one.

I adopted a dog. I let people merge into my lane.
When sunrise sprawls across the horizon,

I'll fill the empty bowl of morning with orange
sky and bird song, go out and make a day of it.

Space Is Silent

Driving home, I'm tempted to keep going
around the bend, beyond the line of trees. Someplace far away
moons are forming in a disk of cosmic dust around
       a distant exoplanet.
Lonely waits in quiet so loud it screams

around the bend, beyond the line of trees, someplace far away
the sun is setting on a day that's gone nowhere.
Lonely waits in quiet so loud it screams.
Scientists say we may soon extract energy from black holes.

The sun is setting on a day that's gone nowhere.
Mercury is shrinking.
Scientists say we may soon extract energy from black holes.
I want something more tonight than listening to the cat crunch
       brown Purina stars.

Mercury is shrinking,
and moons are forming in a disk of cosmic dust around
       a distant exoplanet.
I want something more tonight than listening to the cat crunch
       brown Purina stars.
Driving home, I'm tempted to keep going.

Start With Beautiful

I.

Lavender blossoms in a terra cotta pot, a real pot,
red clay, with cracks and sweet crumbles, lovely
imperfections holding these beauties.
I don't remember planting them.

II.

There she was: bright yellow bird,
deep black wings, sitting in the bottlebrush bush,
and I knew it was a sign from Grandma.
Just as I knew I'd have a boy. Each time.
Just as I knew the biopsy would be positive for breast cancer.

III.

I still fold laundry like my grandmother taught me:
arms wide holding sheets, hands meet in the middle,
and always, same as she did, the long stare
looking at nothing but a window full of sky.

IV.

When I was seven, I believed in Mom and Dad
and the Holy Ghost. That child heart, crisp and clean,
lodged in my chest like another life.

Thursday Afternoon, Last Week

A snowy egret popped into my garden,
stood in the purple sage and stared at me

as I sat in my splintered Adirondack chair making lists.
An unlikely visitor—the lagoon is two miles west—

he had long black legs, silly yellow clown feet,
a few stray plumes sticking straight up

like he forgot his hairbrush this morning.
Our mockingbird swooped and lunged

and the egret blinked, then continued his stare.
Crows perched in palms across the street,

and the dog settled at my side. The bird
lingered twenty minutes or so, a statue.

The yard filled with the hush of low tide
at dusk while the marine layer floated in.

He flapped his wings twice, flew stark white
into the sky, his feet a kite's tail of yellow.

City of Angels

O, Los Angeles, City of Angels,
California's sequined gem, my home-
coming queen, The Town of Our Lady

the Queen of the Angels—I grew up
in her sprawl, played hop scotch
and dodge ball in her cradled basin.

She is Smog Queen, Traffic Queen,
mother of us all: Dodgers, Lakers,
Clippers, and Kings. Los Angeles,

queen of icons: Norms, Bob's Big Boy,
and Winchell's Donuts. Home to
Olvera Street, the Miracle Mile, Holly-

wood stars. She is Guerilla Tacos,
Musso and Frank Grill, pastrami
at Canter's. She's tug boats in the harbor,

Catalina on a clear day. My Lady
of the Angels is skyscrapers, back-
yard chickens, a slog of red taillights

through the valley. She is plum-smudged
sunsets, a harvest moon over Capitol
Records, the city where I learned how

to parallel park, navigate downtown's
four level interchange, how to be a person—
one of many. My town of Our Lady

the Queen of Angels is a twenty-four hour,
red-hot-neon legend that never fades.
Swing by. The porch light is blinking.

Twelve Little Mood Boosters for Troubling Times

Two magenta pinwheels twirling in the morning breeze
Finally seeing a bird splish-splashing in the birdbath
Click clack of word sounds like lickety-split and top-flight dandy
Whoosh of air as a train speeds through the station
Pollywogs: an entire life cycle in a scoop of pond slime
Scent of woodsmoke and warm syrup in the beach campgrounds
Red-eyed tree frogs
Swish of a basketball through the net
Owls soft hoot-hooting each other in the wee hours
A pink hopscotch grid chalked on the sidewalk
Avocado toast
One stray strand of tinsel dangling from a maple tree in July

Hallelujah This Sky

Working downtown today, clouds
in every window of the high rise
across the way: big billowy puffs
vast enough to house God

and sweet baby Jesus, all of heaven's
angels and saints. I'm telling you,
it's a miracle sky, sky in a Bible,
sky so gorgeous it can fix anything

that ails you, and it's reflected
in every single window
on all twenty-four floors of the building
across from me, a colossal glass cloud

there to behold. The attorneys drone:
question, answer, question, answer.
I take down every *do you recall, isn't it true,*
pursuant to, but I want to stop

the deposition and applaud this sky.
Hallelujah this sky. Devour this sky.
Stuff myself with pure white fluffiness,
slip clouds into their transcript.

Redistribution

The history of us sags on the bookshelves: wedding
album, candles, encyclopedias from a time
Pluto was a planet and you still loved me.
You've got a let's-be-civilized list, yours and mine.
Well, watch out. I'm keeping the comfy couch
and the fuzzy maroon blanket, the old dog, and all the kids'
photos. You can have the forks and dishes and half
the untamed hedges. But the cupcakes on the counter—
those are mine. As are the raspberries in the meadow
and the whirligig summer stars. The music in the creek,
the coffee, the apples, the ripe avocado: mine.
I'm keeping the moment under a street lamp
and the quiet beauty of dusk crawling into the yard.
Take your bottle-in-a-paper-bag mess of excuses. Stuff
your six-packs, the cat-clawed chairs, and empty gift cards,
thirty years of rubble into your good-bye U-Haul.
I don't need your casual "sorry." I've got rebar in my soul.

Going Nowhere

As I drag the dog past the local saloon,
the smell makes me think of red vinyl booths
and sad afternoons. I see old men

on tall stools with their elbows on the bar,
circles of smoke like halos above their heads.
And I wonder what will happen to me

as I get older. What if I run out of money
and live in a motel like the one down the street.
One of those places with *Kitchens*, apostrophe *s*.

Or maybe I'll settle down in a silver Airstream
trailer with three wooden steps pushed up
to the door. A place tucked into the corner

of somebody's backyard on a square cement
patio, a hanging cracked plastic parrot
that falls every time a Santa Ana wind

blows dust and leaves into town, a wind
that pushes me this side of crazy.
I'll work in a chair re-caning shop

that's dirty and feels like a stopped clock,
end up playing cards with locals from the bar,
men named Skeeter and Chip, women who walk

to the liquor store in stained terry cloth slippers
to buy their morning rum. Maybe I'll start
forgetting things. At first they won't be important

like how to use chopsticks or spell February,
but one day I might look at an orange
and think lemonade or it could be

the other way around. My sons will visit
less often and never with their wives. They'll tell me
they're busy or have an appointment,

but I'll see it in their eyes, the way they look
through the slanted blinds at the sun, the way
they sit on the edge of a chair.

Wind Season in Los Angeles

Early October afternoon, an eerie
stillness settles over the city, a creepy edginess that

prickles your ears and feels like waiting
in the principal's office. Even kids know

there will be wind after sunset—Santa Anas that howl
all night under an orange moon, devil

winds raging down the canyons to the coast
toppling trees, snapping power

lines, snarling traffic. Meteorologists explain
reduced relative humidity, positive ions, gust velocity,

but never mention the exhilaration swirling
in the air, the mesmerizing waves

rippling through the long grass, the desire
to follow that wild frenzy up and over the hills.

Leaving Blue

So sad the last
few years. All blue gray
like I guzzled foggy days.
This morning's poem will have
the crunch of gold sun,
maybe some purple chaos
zipping through it. The scent
of sea and woodsmoke,
gardenias blooming near
the window. The vanilla taste
of a kiss and all I've missed.
Let dusk fill my porch
with its lonely lament.
I won't be there to hear it.

Feels Like Home

I watch a full moon
bloom high and bright
in the dark, and I want

something simple
but hard to name—coffee
in two cups, the smell

of fresh-cut grass floating
through Sunday, morning
glories growing blue

on the porch. Someone
to pass the salt, water
the flowers, hog the remote.

A reason for dishes.
You wash, I'll dry.
I'm sick of paper plates.

The Accidental Courage of Our Lives

Mom, there are termites in the garage. I can see
their fine dust droppings and I should call someone
to fix it before I come home to a huge pile

of crumbled house and yet week after week I don't.
Work is hard and there's too much of it, and some days
there's not enough of me left to spread on a cracker.

I'm doing that thing again: telling myself life
will be better when I retire, when I organize my stuff,
when I walk three times a week, but that's crap

thinking, I know. Life is right now. I ended up
with the same cancer as you, Mom, and because
you died young, I thought I would, too, but I'm still here,

and that's something: living with the termites,
our doddering old dog, lovely chaos of family.
Living with gratitude for all I thought I'd miss:

daughters-in-law, grandkids' small hands, a little house
with grass to mow and trashcans I lug to the curb
every Wednesday, the beautiful gift of each day—people

to feed, dishes to wash, laundry to fold. On my porch,
gray stems of the plant you gave me reach around the corner,
tiny coral flowers seek sun, want light, want it all.

No More Lonely White Moon

I'm walking away from
slanted sunlight in empty rooms,
leaving the sad and all

its moody blue, trying out
ooh la la and a leap of leopards,
hogs in yellow slickers, wisps

of birds in wind-driven rain.
I'm playing with oomph
and hootie hoo, writing them

into lines like tiny paper umbrellas
slipped into blended drinks.
I've moved on to purple thistle

dotting the hills, strange language
of swampy ponds, a spray of red
trumpet vine framing my window.

Starting From Scratch

For reasons that no longer matter,
I chose to start over, moved to a small town

bordered by fences draped in purple and pink
bougainvillea, a town defined by the sea:

surfboards leaning against walls and wet suits
dripping from porch railings into pots of red

geraniums. I lived six blocks from the edge
of land and water in a place I couldn't afford,

but I needed to know where I was. Some days
I knew I was home only because the key fit

in the door and bills in the mailbox were addressed
to me. I walked miles and miles of sand, watched

surfers and dolphins and whales, collected shells,
and fell in love with the scent of ocean mist

and beach fires. I learned the sea turns rusty
brown just before storms, that June feels like

the inside of a pot lid, that I can count
on the tides and the beauty of a thin strip

of salmon pink hovering above the horizon.
Sometimes there is a green flash at sunset.

Signs Point to Yes

If you need to know, nothing like a Magic 8 ball
for a swift "very doubtful" or "it is decidedly so,"

but if you prefer wending your way into answers,
watch for keys, a feather in your path, red envelope

in the mail. Light your sage green candle, read
page four in three poetry books and find the words

that speak to you. Shuffle your Mother Mary cards
and trust Our Lady of Passion's promise she'll send

what you need. Thank your lucky charms for family,
shelter, health, and all those yellow plumeria blooms.

It's a big sloppy world, but look, you have honeybees
circling a cluster of daisy weeds in your yard.

Forgotten Language of Dreams

Your letter said you'd arrive by train
when midnight is brushed white with moon.
I waited. I waited a century. Morning came
with a sigh. Silver sorrow, empty spoons
whirling wild. Sadness idling on the stairs,
straining pockets, patched over holes. Baby blue,
moody blue, sky blue sheets stretched across
a chilly lake bed. Red rose petals tossed
into the air. Days, months from now,
I'll still be combing them from my hair.

Alternatives

I wonder, when I travel, what it would be like
to live near the lake I'm visiting, the mountains,

the pond, the waterfall. I think about a life
three blocks north of tourist row, tucked into a small

gray house, close enough to bike to my office,
or maybe a shop—a boutique nursery with exotic flowers.

On vacation, I like to wander through neighborhoods,
browse used book stores, imagine myself standing in line

at the movie theater watching dusk creep across the sky.
And in these musings, far from home, I'm alone,

rock climbing or hiking through redwoods, wading
in low tide before settling down to write poetry, too busy

to meet my husband, have my children. There's no need
for more than an occasional friend sitting across a dinner table.

I do think, perhaps, one evening I might look up from my book
with a feeling there's something I've forgotten to do.

Spot of Color

Days now, mockingbirds
have been weaving a nest
near the front porch. They flit
back and forth carrying bits
of string and lint. This morning,
a bird on the fence, curl of pink
in its beak: my granddaughter's
lost hair ribbon.

The End of Me

I'm not one to go visiting grave sites—
just as well, since Mom and Grandma and Grandpa
opted for cremated remains in niches way up high

near the bug zapper, and poor Dad was scattered
in the desert, which is what he wanted, but it worries me.
He's all alone out there in the wind and the heat.

I need a plan for myself or I'll spend eternity
in a cardboard box wedged in my son's car trunk.
If my husband's still around he'll take custody of me,

but he never puts anything away: shoes tucked
under the bed, reading glasses on top of a book.
I'll end up a small cone of ashes next to a bronze urn,

a pile that shrinks with every gust and breeze
until one afternoon the light will hit just right
and he'll dust me off with his sweater sleeve.

Do the Silver Cartwheel

Pretend all is well.
When nightly news says otherwise,

find solace in the iris
popping up in the junkpile of winter

yard a month early. Fall in love
with its purple petals

and delicate light stripes,
the bright yellow fan

plunked smack in the middle
of its blossom like an egg yolk.

Be amazed at its audacity
to bloom no matter the weather.

Emulate the iris.
Jump off the boat, stand on your head,

sing to the carrots and parsley.
Waltz down the bakery aisle.

Do the silver cartwheel.
Flower. Be the bloom: ivory, violet,

ruby-tipped. Leave your petals
in the doctor's office, pack a few

into a loved one's lunch,
fling some out the sunroof.

Strew those posies.
Leave a garland trail.

Most Nights

He washes, and I dry
and stack the plates,

a pleasing mix of his and mine.
I dry his blue mug, chipped from

years before, and my flowered cup,
put away the forks and spoons, slide

the sharp knives into their wooden slots,
match the pots with lids. It's taken some

years, this merging of things, becoming
us—switching sides of the bed, chores,

combining accounts. Odd to be adjusting
lifetime habits at this age, but there's new

things, too, things I've never done with anyone:
sharing grandkids, beach walks, gray hair.

He takes the dish towel from my hand, dries
the kettle, fills it with water for tomorrow's coffee,

then reaches up to wipe steam off the window
above the sink until the two of us reappear.

Welcome Back

Spring burst through the first
lockdown—birds, oh my, the birds
sang night and day, grass greened,

lupine and poppies bloomed galore,
and tiny finches nested in hedges
outside the glass patio door.

We watched nature cycle through
its rhythms as our own went haywire:
cooped up, penned in, shut down.

The season's star was a yellow surprise,
a wild snapdragon that plopped into
an empty spot and flowered all summer,

gone in early fall. Now, a year later,
it's back, settled in place,
just like family home for dinner.

II.

There's a Nest in the Purple-Flowered Tree

Sore throats and ear infections, stomach
flu, dislocated collar bones, one broken arm,

chickenpox, a brain tumor, injuries on bikes,
skates, Flexi-flyers, car accidents, trampled-on

feelings, and from none of these was I able
to protect my children despite my vigilance,

so yes, I understand the mockingbird's
fierce guarding—his swoop from the roof

to nip the dog's ear, racing across the brick
fence when we open the gate by the tree—

those are his babies he's keeping safe,
and he has yet to find it's impossible.

I can send the dog out back, and we can
use our side entrance, but I can't help him

with the hawk crouched on top
of the lamp post or the crows circling the yard.

There will always be a cat
sitting beneath the purple-flowered tree.

Quite Likely a Cerebellar Astrocytoma

the neurosurgeon says, looking at the MRI,
and I think of glowing stars and celestial

bodies, but this is a nine-syllable tumor
embedded in my son's brain. He explains

the stages, slow growing and high grade,
surgery and possible losses: speech,

vision, balance—he calls them deficits,
a word that feels like a plastic glove.

He gives percentages: fifteen, twenty-five,
forty—numbers floating in the air. I want

that moment a week ago standing
in my sunny yellow kitchen holding

the last two slices of whole wheat bread,
just enough to make a grilled cheese

sandwich, half for me, half for my boy,
simple math I understood.

My Heart Is a Shattered Windshield

Four o'clock on a Wednesday afternoon, I've driven
three hours to a Best Western in the crappy part of town
for my son's doctor appointment in the morning.
The desk clerk asks if I'm here on business or pleasure.

I look at the mangled Vons grocery cart in the empty parking lot
through smudges on the glass lobby door. "Pleasure," I say,
but the truth is neither. Untreated, my son's life expectancy
is two point eight years. His disease can be managed,

but not cured, and the cost of medication is near impossible.
The truth is we've waited thirteen months for insurance
approval to see this specialist. The truth is I'm a howling
windstorm of fear—my boy's just barely thirty.

I don't yet know there is hope, that tomorrow the doctor will reach
into a drawer and toss my son a six-thousand-dollar miracle drug,
a bottle of pills lobbed across his desk like a red and yellow
beach ball sailing through a shimmering summer sky.

When We Mistake Windows for the Sky

Usually we leave the stunned birds
outside, but that crow is watching

and the injured wren has no chance
without our help. We bring her

inside tucked into a deep box
loosely covered for the night.

This morning she's perched on
the kitchen table as though waiting

for us, like a happy baby
eager to be lifted from a crib.

We pop out the window screen
and shepherd the bird back into

her world of trees and sky. Each time
I plop a spider, lizard, roly-poly bug

outside, I think about the giant girl
in the Twilight Zone episode playing

with toy humans. The universe is vast
and wondrously odd, and one day

a dinosaur-sized insect might pluck me
from my bed and set me down alone

in the desert. If karma is true,
there will be a bowl of water nearby.

Sentinel Node

The dye moves to the first node the cancer
goes to if it has spread. That's the sentinel node,
the one we'll remove during surgery and send
to pathology, the one we hope comes back clear.
                                        —Dr. T

Six a.m., low tide, sun rising
into a glorious sky. I watch
two sandpipers outrun a wave.

I've come to hear the ocean,
not listen to a homeless beach bum
talk about rocks and shells

and glittering sand in his pockets.
"Do you want to see?" he asks.
I tell him, "No, thank you."

He shuffles off and I head home.
Later that morning, lying on a table
in nuclear medicine, I watch a tech

shoot radioactive dye into my breast.
"Here's where I injected you,"
she says. "And here," she points

to the monitor "is your sentinel node."
The white dot on the screen looks like
the first star in a blue-black dusk.

I stare at it, that star, afraid of what's inside.
I wonder if I should have said yes
to the man on the beach. I wonder if

I should have said yes to everything.

Counting

Three days past Christmas, the hospital walls are still
decorated with holiday cheer—snowflakes, reindeer,
a wreath with a crumpled candy bar wrapper

stuffed into the artificial evergreen. Torn magazines,
empty cups, and old newspapers litter the tables.
The TV is tuned to the weather channel, sound muted.

A wilting silver get-well balloon sways in the corner,
its long ribbon snaking curlicues across the floor. It bobs
like a welcoming committee when anyone passes by.

We sit in orange plastic chairs counting linoleum squares—
seventeen across, twenty-one up and down, all of them
dusky green with gold swirls except one gray replacement

near the vending machine. We count fluorescent flickers,
trying to time them, see if there's a pattern. Long, short, short.
We count the PA announcements and ping of elevator doors.

We count slats in the dirty beige window blinds. There are nineteen.
Two are bent on the right. One dips in the middle. We count
what we'd give up—everything—to hear the word benign.

Tuesday Morning Is When I Find Out

The doctor talks about pathology,
stages and grades. I'm thinking about
my grandson, too young to remember me.
I wonder if I'll be here when the new baby comes.

I ask for a copy of the biopsy report.
At home I sit in bed with my computer
looking up words. I'm afraid the cancer
has spread, that the surgeon will slice open

my breast and find a gray snarled mess
inside my chest. I'm afraid
it's invaded every node, is racing up
and down my spine, devouring organs,

that my sons will write "Mom" on tribute
signs they'll carry in fundraiser walks.
The doctor told me the tumor
could have been growing five to eight years.

I picture it climbing aboard and nestling in,
living close to my heart—there when I met
my husband, when I first held my grandchild—
a silent witness to my life.

Escape to Moon Palace

Zebra G nibs, oblique pen holders,
Moon Palace ink—a list of yummy supplies.

I'm tempted to run off Saturday mornings
and learn calligraphy. English Round Hand,

the catalogue says. Just leave the laundry and dishes,
ignore Carol starting chemo, Pat and her pain pump,

all the rest—there's a lot of us in the cancer support group.
I picture dipping my pen in ink, following the arrows

down, up, around, rows of letters, learning to write
thinking of you, sending good thoughts,

mailing a card—something more solid than hope,
which fades like flowers left too long in a vase.

Not Yet, My Grandchildren Aren't Ready

No matter the number of fingers crossed, or the love
and bright shining hope waiting for me in the lobby,

the scooch from gurney to surgical table is a lonely journey.
Listen up, tumor (the word feels like gristle you pull

from your mouth and set discreetly on the edge
of your dinner plate), you can take chunks of the breast

or the whole thing if you want. Heck, you can have both.
But please, leave me my liver, stay away from the brain—

your favorite haunts. I have yet to show Gracie how to
thread the old Singer, teach Jack to drive a stick shift,

take them on a grunion run. I'm not done embedding
myself in the marrow of their sweet growing bones.

Afternoons With Ray

Dr. O, you told me to show up four o'clock sharp,
seven weeks, Monday through Friday. You said

you'd compute a path around my heart, I'd be tired,
but nothing would hurt. You didn't tell me how cold

that treatment room is, how exposed I'd feel climbing
onto the table every day, techs using my new blue tattoos

as maps to manipulate me into position. You didn't tell me
they'd close the heavy door and leave me with Ray,

(I named your machine), that he would lumber up and over,
his unblinking eye staring at me from all angles. And now,

seven weeks have passed, there's nothing left to do but hope.
I miss you, Dr. O. I think I'm afraid to be alone.

Status: Post Left Breast Carcinoma

Oh, magnificent void.
It's me, member 37295.
I'm adrift in the vast
blundering indifference
of managed healthcare.
Somewhere inside the abyss
is the radiologist's report.
I need those results.
Please, take my call.
Keep me on hold.
Let me pretend that you care.

Oncology Waiting Room

Almost to the door, the FedEx guy
walks back toward the receptionist,

plucks a flower from the vase on her desk.
He turns to the woman slumped

in a chair next to mine, kneels to tuck
the yellow daisy into her head scarf.

Faster than she can smile or say thank you,
he's roaring down the street in his truck,

two taps on the horn, leaving me
considering the possibility of angels.

Standing in a Near Empty Parking Lot With My Mammogram Results

The receptionist folds the report in thirds,
slides it into an envelope he seals shut,

and I wonder why not just hand it over;
maybe he knows something I don't yet.

Seagulls swoop and squawk from light posts.
I've read they head inland when rain's on the way,

but the sky looks clear. I hold my breath
and rip the envelope open. I want this report

to shower me with confetti and invite me out
to celebrate. I want this report to belly up to the bar

and order us spicy jalapeno poppers and two beers
to wash them down. I want this report to sloppy kiss me,

take me to the tip top of a Ferris wheel and propose
we go another year. And oh, benevolent universe,

thank you, thank you—my favorite words:
benign findings, my passport into tomorrow.

The Jasmine Wants In

This spring the jasmine outside the bedroom door
is twining across the pittosporum branches,

grabbing stucco and pushing its way inside the house.
I've tried unwinding the tendrils, sending them up

the new trellis but the jasmine's not having it,
just inches back in every night, green shoots tiptoeing

closer and closer. Its relentless quest for the bed
feels familiar and I wonder if the cat's come back

as a vine, a restless soul who needs us still—his death
last year so abrupt, there was no time for good-bye.

We decide to let him be. Next morning, a bouquet
of white stars blooming between us, Gizmo's favorite spot.

Colleen, Say Yes

There's always something
beckoning from the dark path.
Yesterday it was a crow—glossy,

sassy, swooped in and took
the three-day-old hatchling
leaving a shredded nest

and no more doves, no more
fluttering wings under the eaves.
You can get lost in the quiet.

And yet. Orange butterflies
dazzle the yard, morning glories
twine their way through thickets

of wild rose, and the very old dog
asks for dinner. A plane
writes white word puffs across

the afternoon sky: "Marry Me,
Colleen," and I'm hoping Colleen,
whoever she is, says yes.

Alchemy

We knew it could happen—there was no way
that messy house of twigs was safe up there

in our eaves. The nest blew down, and the doves
rebuilt using the sprigs and wisps now on the ground.

Restored, they took turns sitting on the nest—
female at night, male during the day.

One morning, he fluttered in for duty
with a hard landing and the whole thing crashed:

nest, two eggs—smashed.
My grandkids and I buried the bits of shell and goop

in a shallow grave under a tree fern in the yard.
We talked about life and death, the vagaries of nature,

but the next week I had no explanation for the knot
of tiny lavender flowers blooming in that spot.

Sinking

We're in the kitchen, my friend and I,
finishing dinner, drinking wine.
She peels the label,
long messy shreds of paper,

wads it into little tiny clumps.
I take the bottle away,
ask again "What's going on?"
Louder, like maybe she didn't hear me

the first time. She runs her fingers
through her hair, barely there.
"It's back," she says.
I sit, stunned. Then hand her the bottle,

which makes us laugh.
And it feels good, this laughing.
One moment suspended,
a moon hovering above us.

I ask about chemo,
and she says, "No."
When I realize what that means,
I shake my head, again and again

as though the truth can't lodge
if I stay in motion. I get up
to load the dishwasher—forks,
spoons, plates all in their place.

When there's nothing left to do,
I move my chair closer to hers,
and we sit holding hands
as the little boat of her life sinks.

Coasting Downhill

On the way home from chemo
we're stopped at the long red light
at Roscoe and Reseda, both of us
looking at the roadside shrine.
It was bigger a year ago.
Now, the cross is gone,
the fresh flowers have been replaced
with plastic ones, and the pinwheel is stuck.
As we drive past, Cheryl says,
"Don't forget me."
I pat her hand and try not to cry.
Five months later her ashes sit
in a vase on her husband's dresser,
it too a small shrine. To its left
is a photo taken just a year ago—
Cheryl's coasting downhill on her daughter's bike,
gold and silver streamers sailing behind.
She's laughing and waving.
Already saying good-bye.

Migratory Patterns of Yellow Birds

I told her yellow birds were the sign
a miracle was on its way.

I told her because I wanted her to live,
and because I knew the Hooded Orioles

arrive in spring and love the nectar
in the red bottlebrush out front.

She'd come visit and see the birds and believe.
They swarmed the flowers—twelve, ten

flitting in and out, hanging upside down,
filling the tree with chatter, making us laugh.

"Yes," she said, patting my hand, ever the best
friend, "it may be a sign." She passed in June.

Now the orioles are returning south
and brittle red spikes dot the driveway.

Cheryl Checks Into Heaven

Four days of rain and finally, before dawn
it stops. Morning is hot and still and feels like

standing in a slow-moving line. The ocean
is murky brown. I wait till dark and walk down

to the beach. The waves glow, break
iridescent marine. I jump in, kick up sprays

of glittering sea water. Oceanographers say
it's dinoflagellates, an algae bloom, but I slide

through damp sand, and my footsteps sparkle
like sprinkled blue stars. I say it's a sign.

When You Find Something Else

Because I've never used the word
murder in a poem, I fill my purse

with bird seed and roam the hills
looking for crows, climbing a path

through a string of young scrub pines—
no crows, not even a black wing,

but a few feet from trail's end, a wrench
of yellow warblers whirls high into the sky.

III.

Everything Was Going to Be Better

When I graduated, married,
bought a house, paid it off, kids

grew up, husband quit drinking,
divorce stopped aching. Always

waiting. For what I never knew.
Until now. Sitting in this blue chair

in the corner of a crooked rock garden,
impatiens and fuzzy weeds pushing up

between faded chipped brick, sun warm
on my head, I bend to tie

my grandson's shoe, inhale the scent
of sticky sweat and peanut butter,

his hand a small weight on my shoulder
I want to keep forever.

Splintered White Picket Fence

I come from a long line of women
who check for a murderer lurking

behind the shower curtain,
who worry about tetanus and polio,

bees swarming the front porch,
women who passed down their angst,

their strength and independence,
women who taught me well:

if your heart's stuck in a cheese grater,
hide it in the kitchen drawer. Fold your anger

into a napkin and get the kids to school.
Smile through prickly silences and never

ladle family secrets into a stranger's bowl.
Take a small gift when visiting and pay

your own way. Go beyond ordinary
and extend your Sunday best.

Run with scissors if necessary,
and no matter what, say thank you—

write it across the steamy mirror
in the morning and believe it all day.

Normal

Van's singing "Brown Eyed Girl" and I'm remembering
Mike with the strawberry blonde hair. He was my first
kiss, my first St. Christopher to wear. We were fifteen that summer
with nothing to do and no one watching us. Then his mother left
when his sister got sick. His dad moved them home to Iowa.

I saw him again at a funeral. He'd enlisted, married a girl
named Mandi, had a baby on the way. He wanted to come back
from Vietnam and teach junior high, have a normal family.
"You know," he said, "shoot hoops after dinner, mow the lawn
on Saturday, Sunday football." I've heard nothing since.

I could search the internet, but I prefer thinking of him
pushing a lawnmower on a Saturday afternoon, Mandi inside
a bright shiny kitchen filling two glasses with lemonade. She carries
them to the screen door, opens the latch with her elbow, backs out
and catches the handle with a finger so it doesn't bang shut

and wake the baby. She sets the drinks on the porch step.
Mike stops the mower, walks over to join her. They sit in the sun
and quiet. The heat dries the damp circles under the glasses.
A dog barks. A plane drones through a blue untroubled sky.
And the smell of just-cut grass fills the afternoon.

For My Sons, a Few Facts

One minute you're saying, "No, thank you"
to a second helping of sweet potato pie—

a day later, you're a goner. Listen, boys,
tomorrow morning you'll think of things

you wish you'd said. Go, fix what's broken.
Regret is blue and waits in a small room down the hall.

Grandma's Telling Me

Sonnenizio on a line from Ashley Anna McHugh's
"The Unquarried Blue of Those Depths is All But Blinding"

how love's a rust-worn boat,
kind of flaky, how it wants
tending, how I need to brush
away rust, learn how to patch
and paint. And somehow
I lose the connection just how
love is a boat anyhow, but years
pass and I begin to understand how
fragile love is, how much care—
do it right, girl, you'll see, somehow
it floats. And I do, I can see how
love is a boat, how I need to patch
and paint, how much work it takes
to stay on board, how fast rust can flake.

Just Because

Turning the corner, I see a kid.
He's maybe seventeen, nineteen

walking down the sidewalk carrying a bouquet.
They could be for anyone, those flowers,

but I want them to be for his mother.
I want them waiting in a glass vase

on the table when she comes home from work,
a bright orange and purple surprise

lighting up the kitchen just because
she's a good mom and he's a good son.

I think she'll set her purse on the chair,
lean against the faded gray wall

and wipe away tears with her fingertips,
and for a moment he'll stare at a spot

on the floor and wish he'd done nothing at all,
but she'll pull him close with her arm

around his shoulder just long enough to say,
"Thank you," before she lets go.

Katie Asks Why Not Be Optimistic

Listen, Katie, hope is not that easy.
Humanity is a collision of red and blue
chaos, a giant slop of disharmony

that's killing us and the planet. You can't
just order up a box of hope and be an optimist
by noon tomorrow—you've got to create your own.

I learned from the experts:
I sat out front and watched Jack
shoot hoops in the driveway, over and over

and over till he had nineteen in a row, one
more than yesterday. Gracie and I picked
dandelion puffs and blew them into the breeze,

fingers crossed they'll root in the grass.
Let's fill the yard, Grandma, grow wishes
for everyone. All afternoon, we seeded

our future: yellow flowers and fluffy white
globes stretched across a wide green lawn
under a bright chrysanthemum sun.

Stitching

I wish I'd thought to ask
for my mother's sewing box,
the small tin one she was using

near the end, carrying it with her
to doctor appointments, chemo, the hospital,
always stitching while waiting,

pocket-sized creations she framed and gave away:
fancy knots, smiling black spiders dangling
from shiny silver webs, a ladybug perched

on an orange winking sun, Mom's name
embroidered diagonally in the lower left corner—
remember me, remember me.

Question

"Am I the best girl in the world?"
My granddaughter shakes the Magic Eight Ball
with six-year old might and, of course, the answer
is "yes, definitely" because this girl, she's a neon
sparkler. She's fizzy water crackling on ice.
This girl is soccer and flag football, a rainbow
confetti glitter crafter, a singer, a barrier hurdler
speeding into tomorrow. I pray her glow-in-the-dark
heart finds the world's guard rails and keeps her safe
because she's whirling toward the future, one cartwheel
after another, a silver star streaking across the yard.

We See the Past When We Look at Stars

When my boys were young,
I tucked them into bed, folded the blanket

into a "v" to pull up later if the night was cold.
After a story, I kissed their foreheads,

whispered *sleep tight,* and stood at the door
as glow-in-the-dark stars lit up the ceiling and walls.

One by one my sons grew into their own lives.
When the last left for college, I found his good-bye—

one star glowing on the ceiling above my bed.
I took that star, added a galaxy more,

and everywhere I've lived, my portable universe
has been the last to peel off, first to stick on.

Tonight I tucked grandchildren into my bed
under the same star, faint but still glowing.

What's Hidden in DNA

"Oh, a wish, a kiss, some lunar mist" I tell
my granddaughter when she asks what's in the box

on my bedroom shelf. It's a family treasure, pretty,
intricately made, and tucked inside a hidden compartment

is a list of eleven types of wood used to craft it.
I don't know what Grandma's mother kept in it,

but Grandma put her small scissors, the gold ones
that look like a stork, a thimble, and a spool

of black thread inside. Mom and Dad set the box
on the coffee table filled with loose change,

and after the divorce, Mom emptied it. I hand the box
to Gracie and say, "Two hawk feathers, and a secret.

A sand dollar, navy blue button, and the scent of cinnamon."
She lifts the lid, smiles, and says, "Yes, I see."

Some Call It Treasure

Junk toys my grandparents called them,
three bags, one for each boy, filled with stuff

my kids loved: stickers, red caps popped off
whipped cream cans, magnets, corks, rubbery

spiders and lizards, random board game tokens
all dumped across the floor, plastic that poked

bare feet, clogged the vacuum cleaner, spread
through my house. I wonder who had more fun—

little boys sorting through treasure or my grandparents
on the hunt for it all, strolling through Leisure World

looking for bits of sparkle the gardener's broom missed,
stooping to grab a marble or tiny pencil,

crossing a parking lot and spotting a stray
Happy Meal toy, amassing piles of plastic surprises.

When Grandpa died, my sons gave
their great-grandmother a box of dinosaurs,

striped dragons, and an orange frog—
a zoo of creatures to keep her company.

I'm Still Saving a Seat

Those slow hot days of summer before sixth grade,
Bethany and I rode our bikes to mass every morning,

cutting across the empty lot through the curly weed
past the stagnant pond. We sat in the back near the cart

of flickering red candles. Kneeling next to Bethany,
I was in love with our piety, the purity of our conviction,

the sanctity of our mission: we would heal Bethany's mother
with prayer and love. Behind the white stretch of altar, the priest

held up the host and we tapped our eleven-year old hearts
and whispered *amen*. I believed Our Lady would appear one day

and tell us *fear not*. She'd wrap us in her velvety blue cloak
and we'd smell like blush pink roses the rest of summer.

Late August, we huddled in the dark on Bethany's bed
and listened to the thump clump of a gurney wheeling

her mother's body out of the house. Five days later,
we sat holding hands at the funeral. When school started,

I saved a seat for Bethany, but she tapped her heart
and said *I can't* then disappeared into a circle of girls.

Someone's Peeling an Orange

That scent, I can almost taste the tartness.
It smells like summers with Maureen and Abby,

sitting on sun-warmed cement steps, sticky
juice dripping down our chins and arms, dodging

red ants and bees, ignoring calls to come in,
laughing at how mothers stretch out a name:

Aaabyyy, but when they yell that third time,
you know they mean it: right now, Missy.

Six o'clock dinner at the small glass table,
kick the can until dark. Before riots, before fires

lit up the L.A. sky, before the air tasted like smoke.
If we'd known, we'd have loved it more.

How to Fold Laundry

Grandma's hands, spotted brown with age,
veins like rivers diverging, always busy.
She's hanging the wash, reaches down
for a damp shirt, clips it onto the line

with a wood clothespin as it begins to rain.
"Just like Guatemala, wet and smells green,"
she says, sniffing the air. I ask if she did
laundry when she lived there. She gathers

dry sheets, drops them into the basket,
looks beyond the yard, past the trees,
and says, "There's laundry everywhere, girl."
In the kitchen, she shows me how to fold

towels, shorts, sort socks and roll them
into balls. We play grocery store. And Go Fish.
She paints my fingernails fuchsia. And clear.
And fuchsia again. I have my grandmother's

piano, her bird books, and the butterfly picture.
I have her hands. And grandchildren of my own.
Thank goodness I kept a copy of her heart:
a red paper cutout sprinkled with glitter.

Wings

I found a two-inch black and white
square picture of a birdhouse high

in a bare winter tree, stark against
the tall snowy mountains. On the back,

in Grandma's writing: "The birdhouse
through our kitchen window, Fairbanks."

I remember her staring out windows,
looking beyond the trees. She preferred

hills to valleys, forest over sea. Was it birds
she loved or the allure of wings. I inherited

Grandma's Steinway and her music.
I've been practicing, following her

penciled marks: "hold pedal," "push forward
on black keys," an asterisk next to "crescendo."

Today swallowtail butterflies fluttered through
Chopin's notes and Grandma's stories

filled the room: rain showers in Guatemala,
northern lights sweeping across an Alaskan sky,

a flock of Steller's jays wheeling above
a meadow of poppies and lupine.

Looking For Hope

We know, America,
what it is to stand alone
in an empty room holding
nothing but a bouquet of sorrows.

To stare at a telephone wire
heavy with birds. Listen
to silence so loud it screams.
We will tire of shoveling

sadness from our beds.
We will look for our spot
on the map. We will find
the sun in a symphony of shadows

and fall in love with light,
the way it shimmers and pours
across the land, the way it sparks
the tender furnace of our hope.

About the Author

Victoria Melekian grew up in Los Angeles, and now lives with her husband in Carlsbad, California. She writes poetry, short fiction and, on occasion, a novella-in-flash. Her work has appeared in print and online and has been nominated for Best of the Net and the Pushcart Prize. She makes quilts, plants flowers, and practices *Canon in D* on the piano. For more, visit her website: victoriamelekian.com

Sheila-Na-Gig Editions

www.ingramcontent.com/pod-product-compliance
Lightning Source LLC
Chambersburg PA
CBHW020800130626
46554CB00006B/2284